MY FIRST HALLOWEEN

CAT

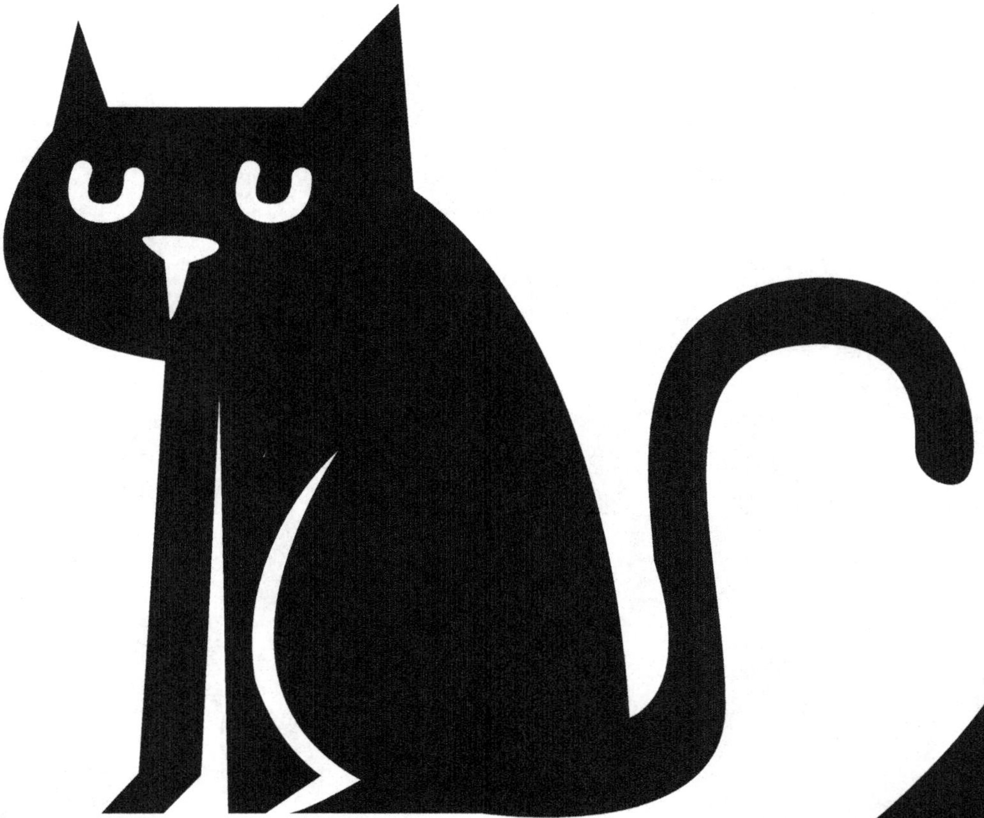

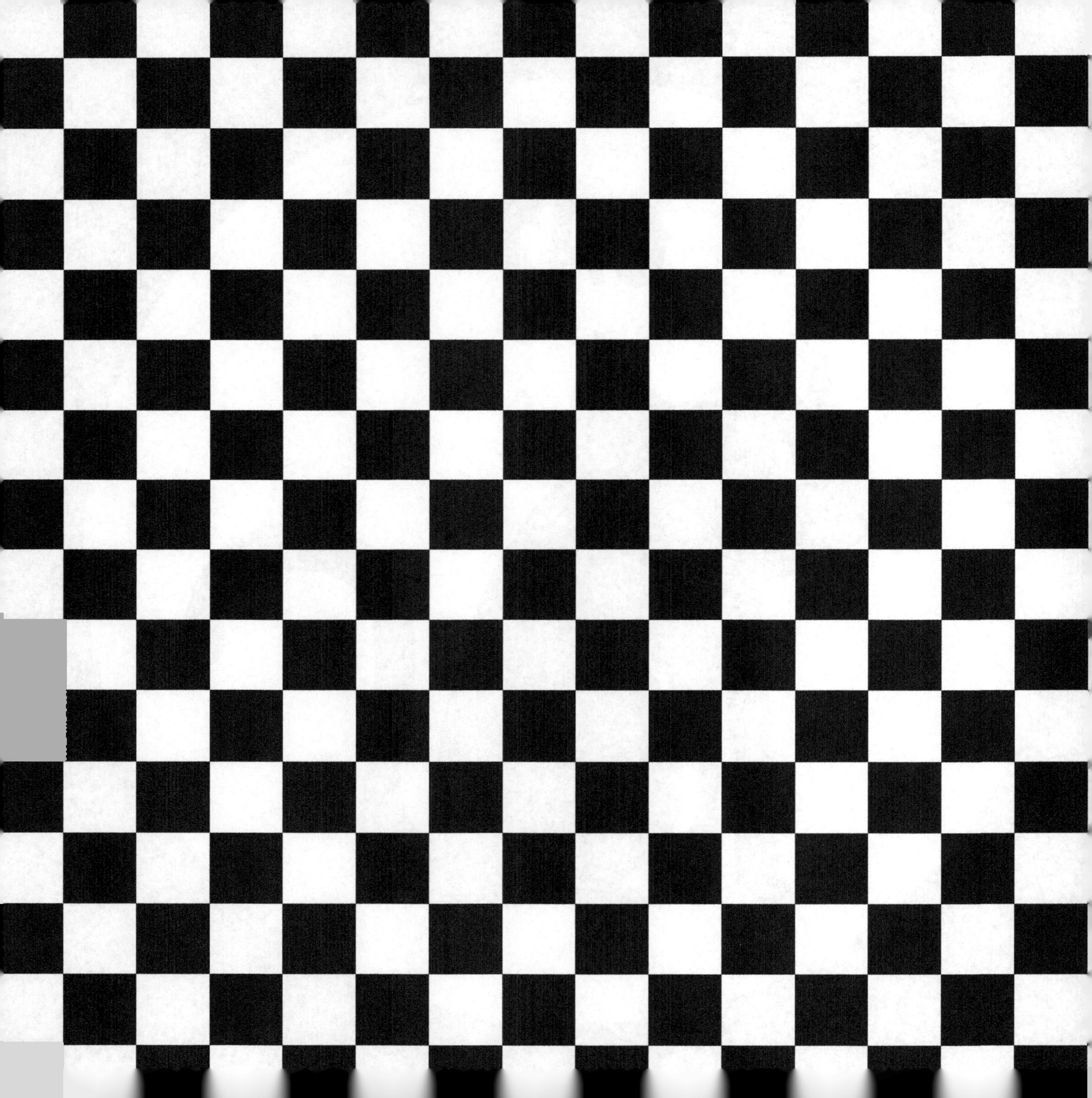

GHOST

PUMPKIN

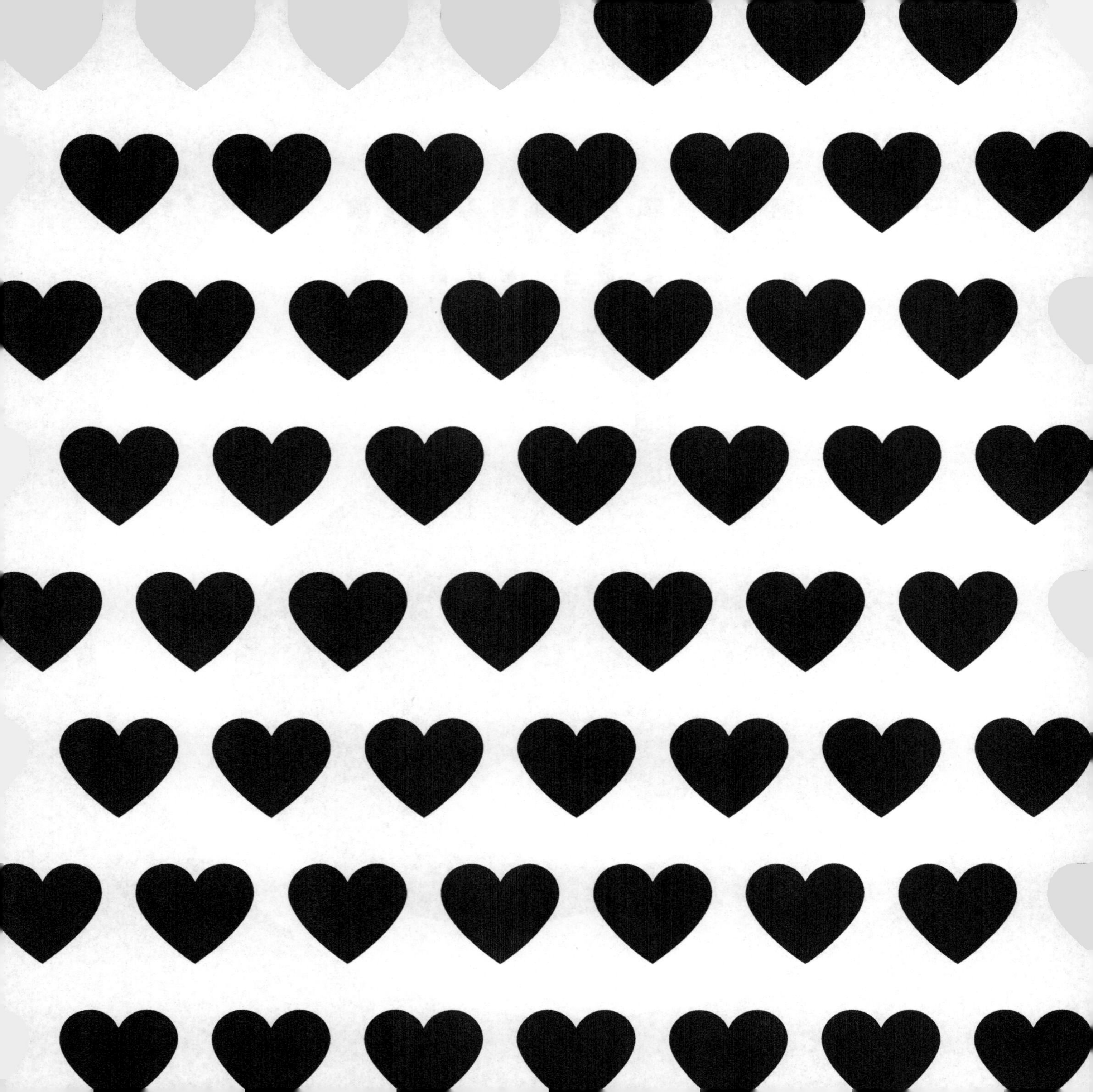

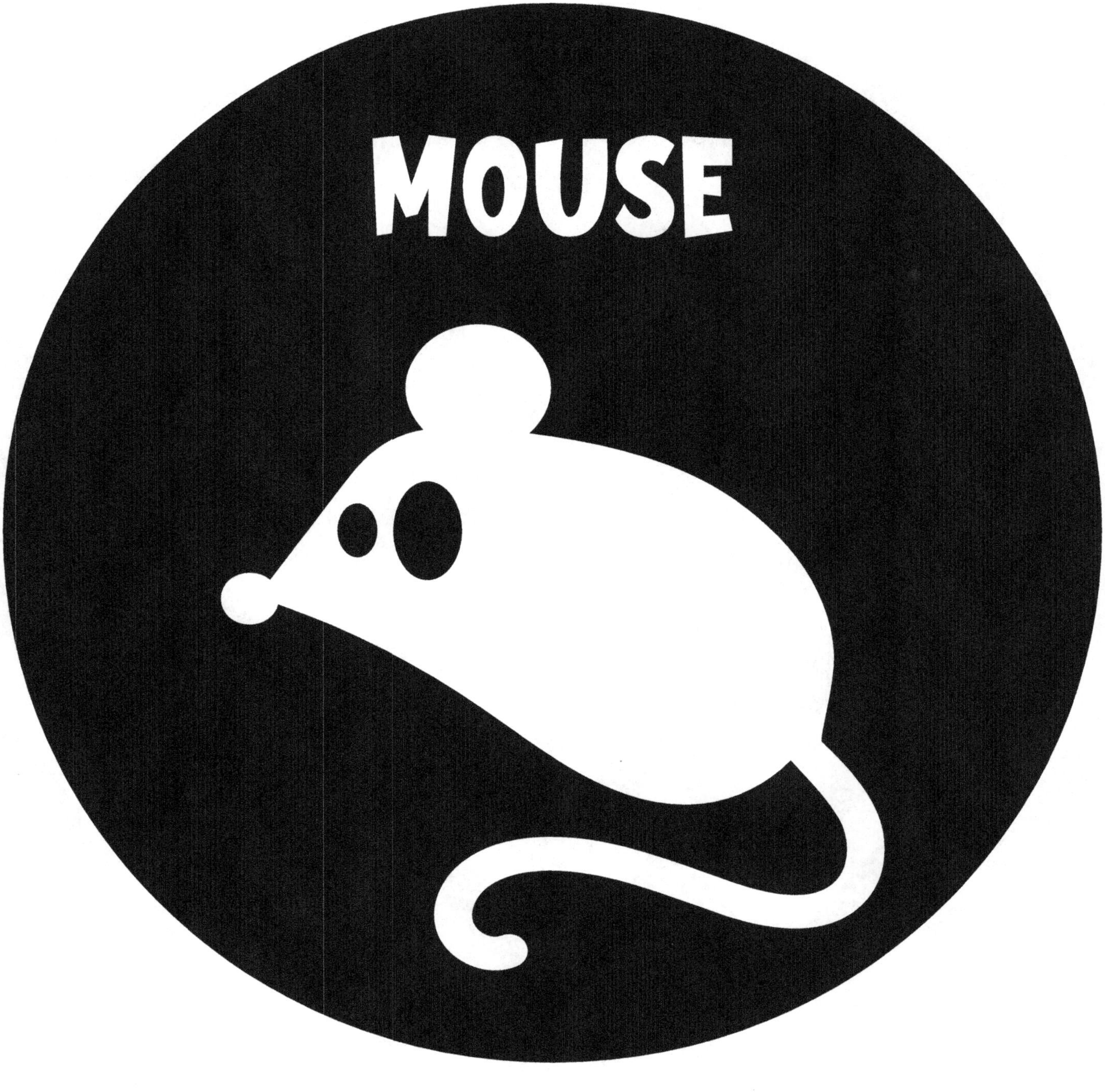
MOUSE

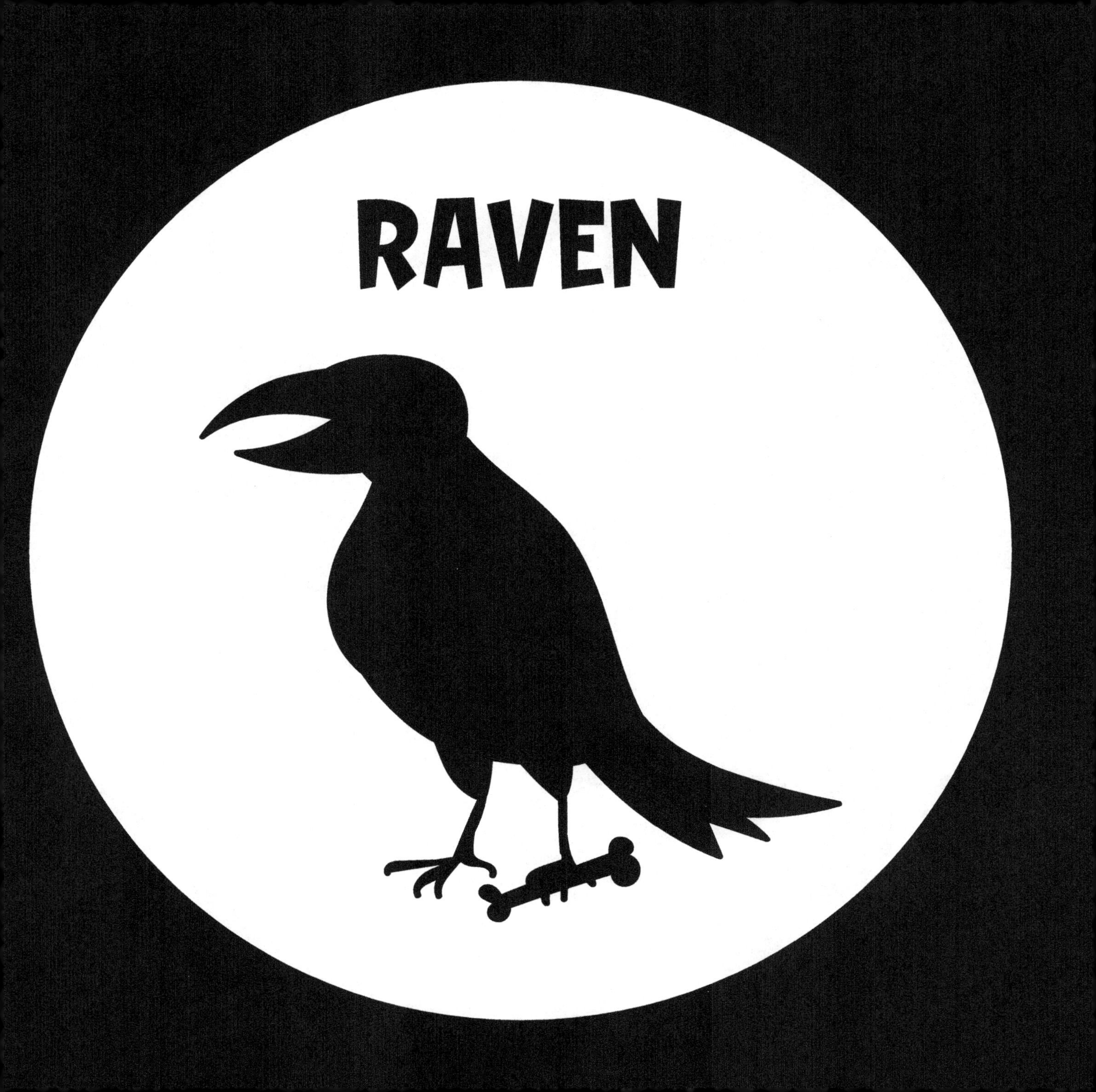
RAVEN

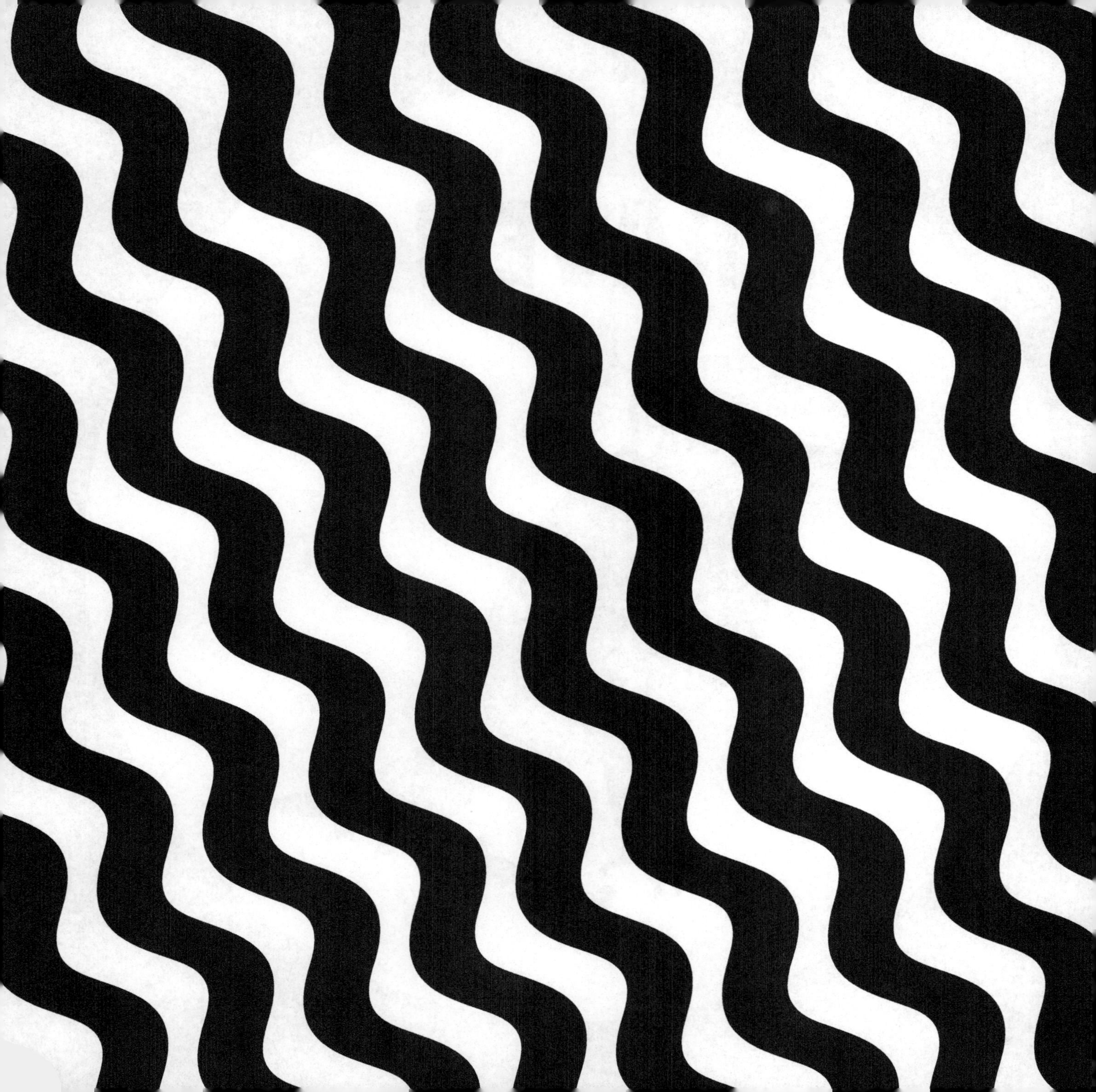

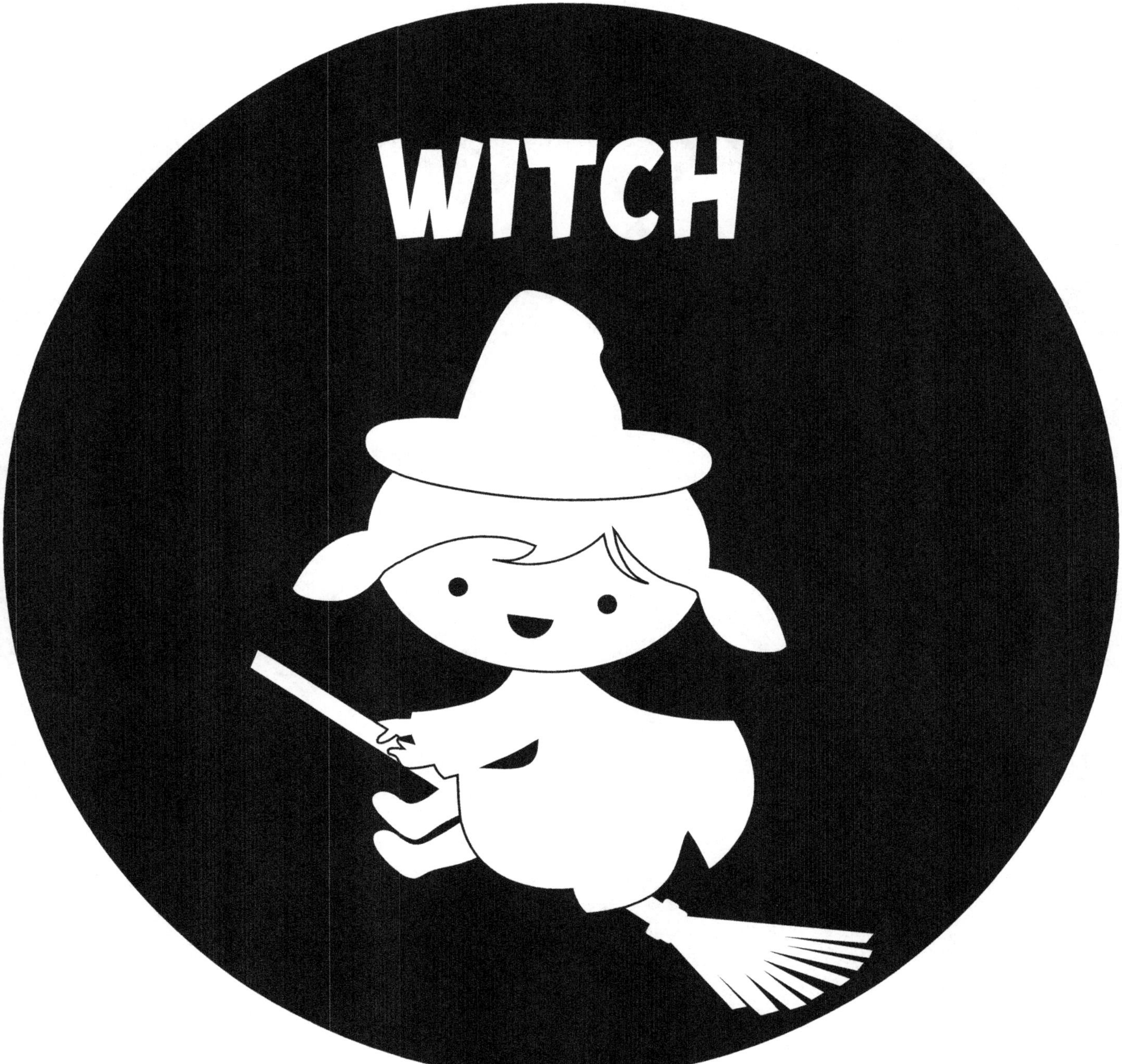
WITCH

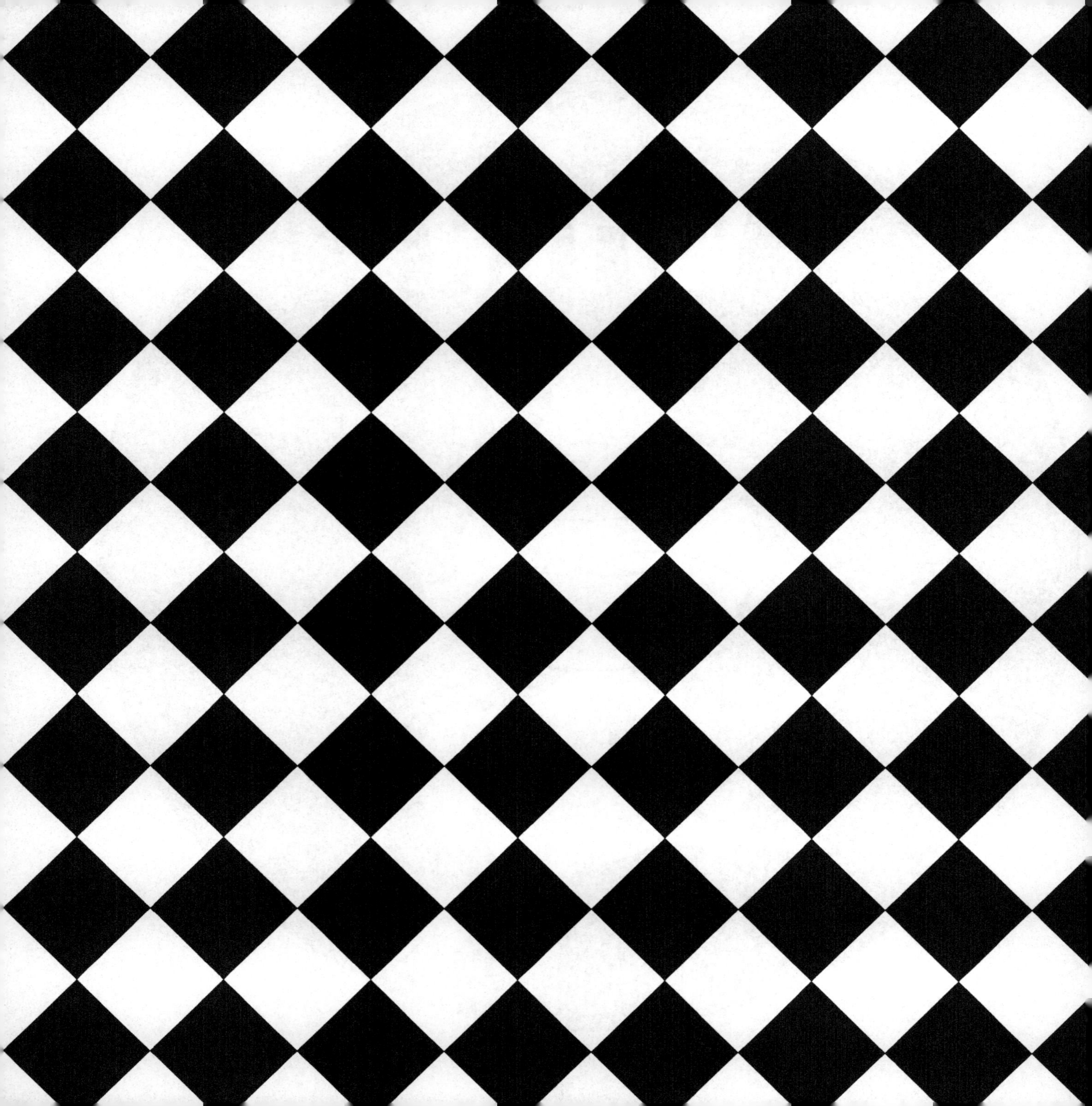

CANDY

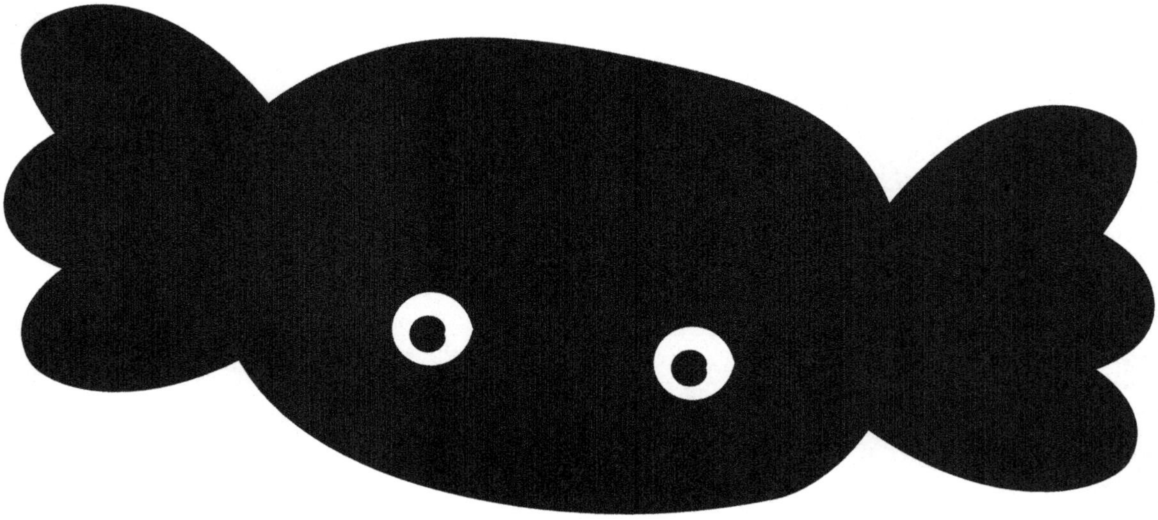

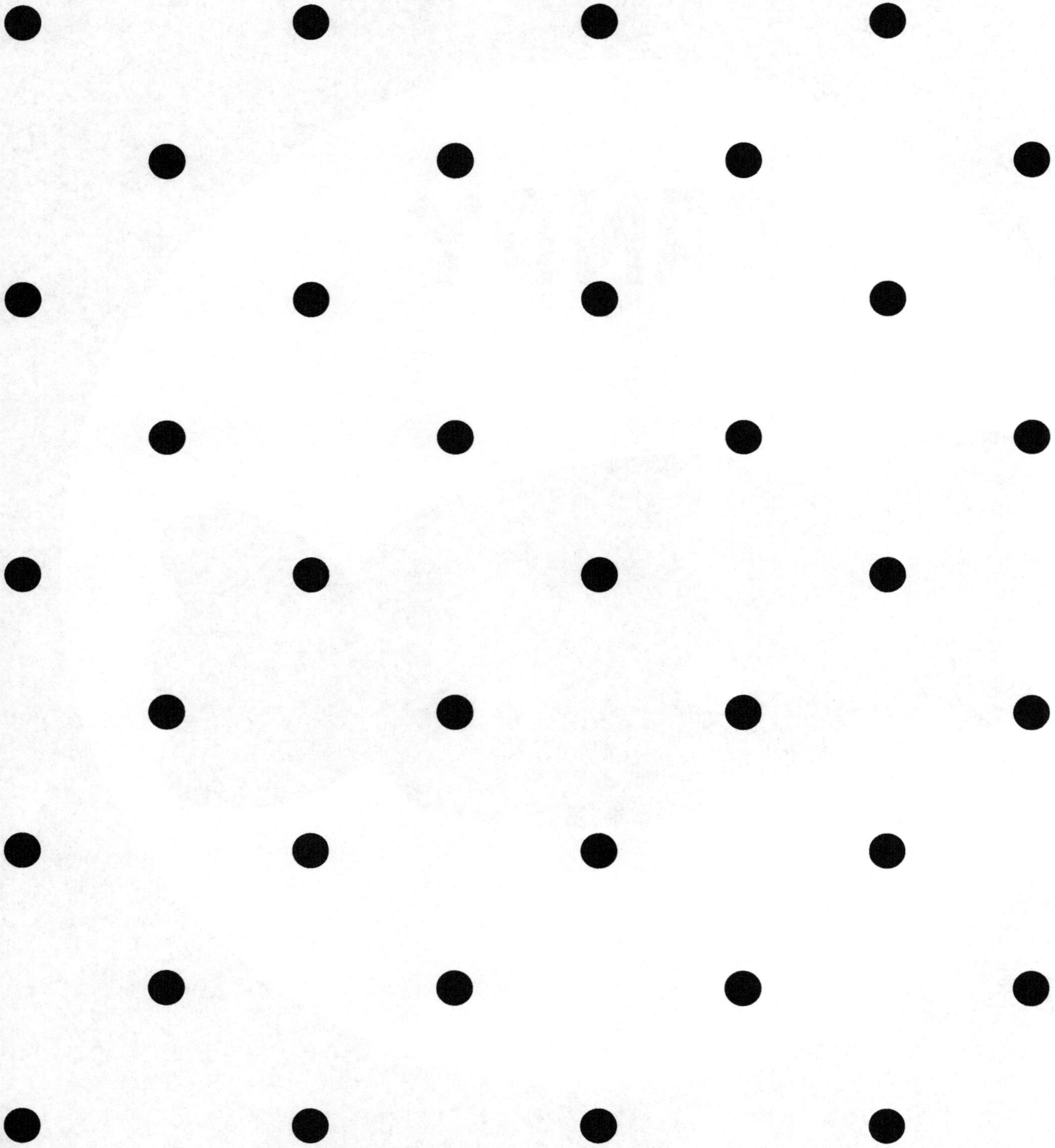

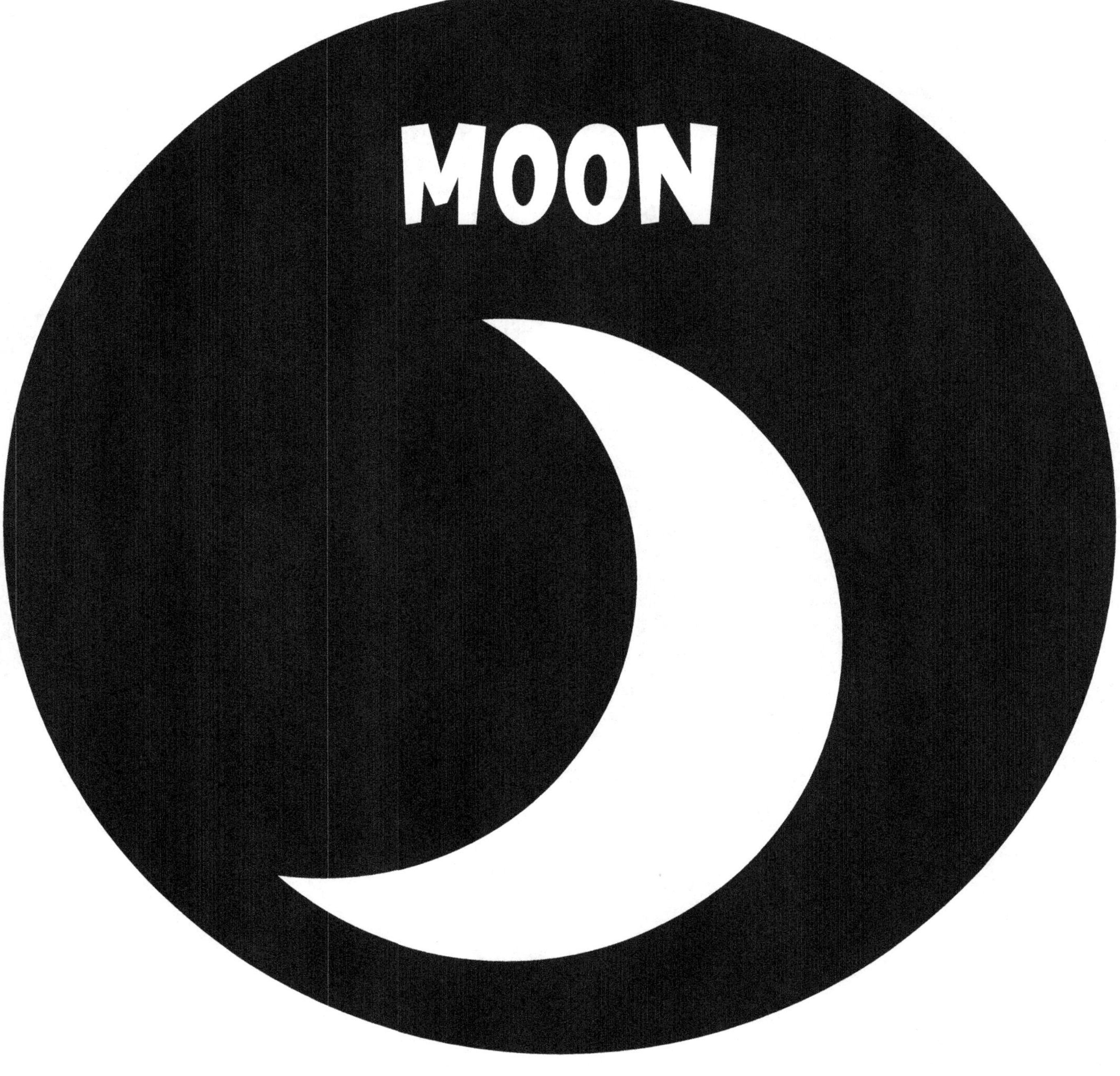
MOON

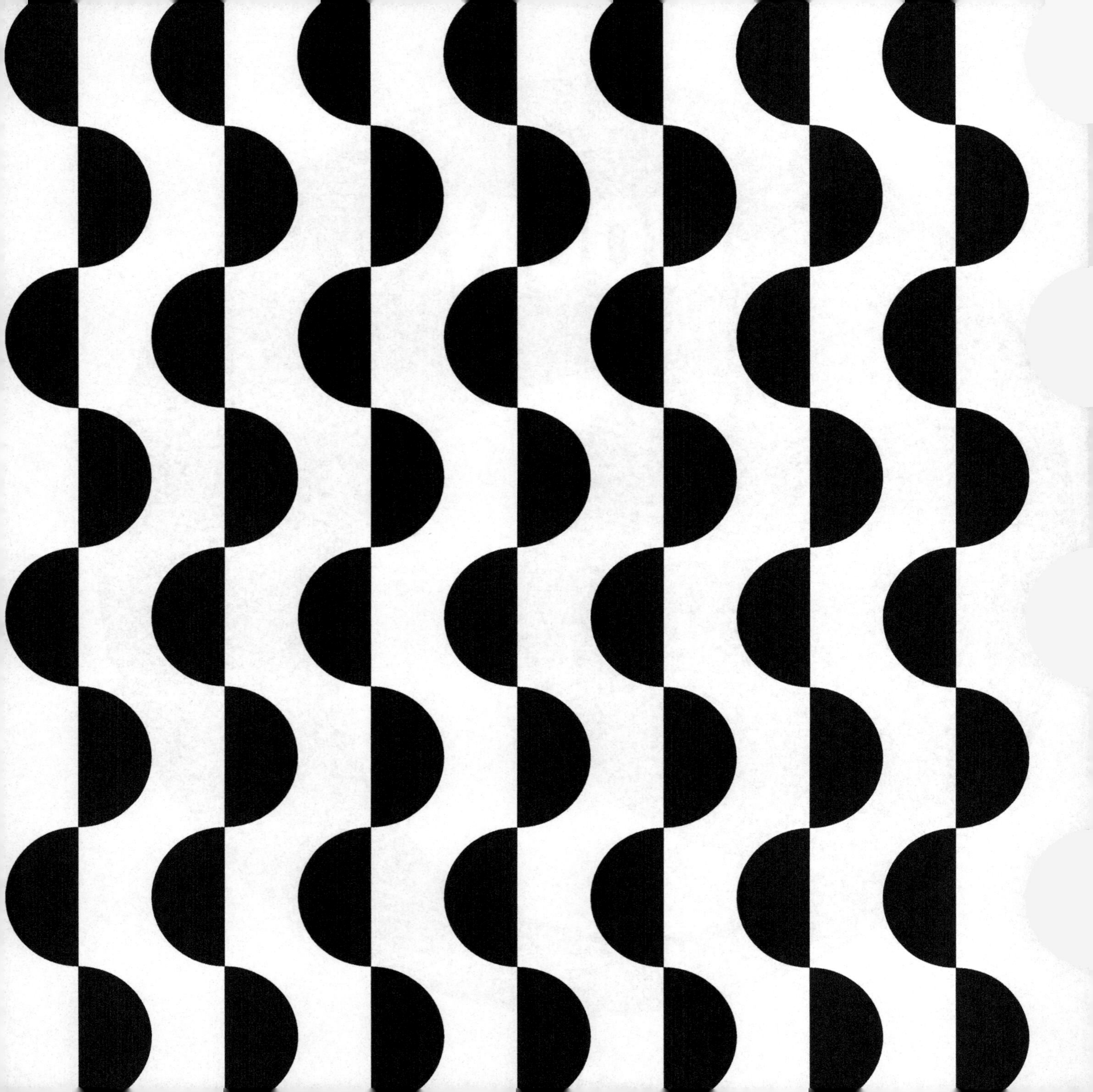

CAULDRON

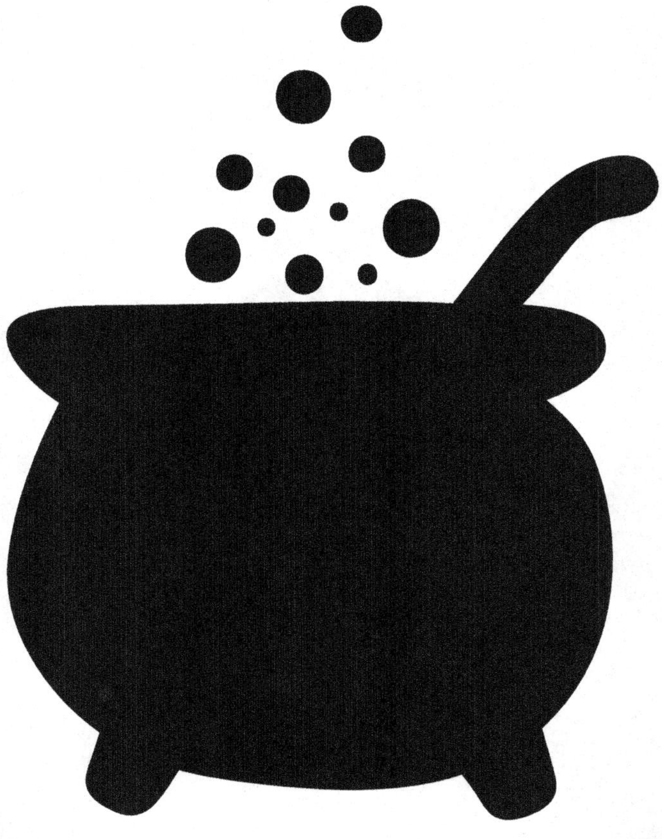

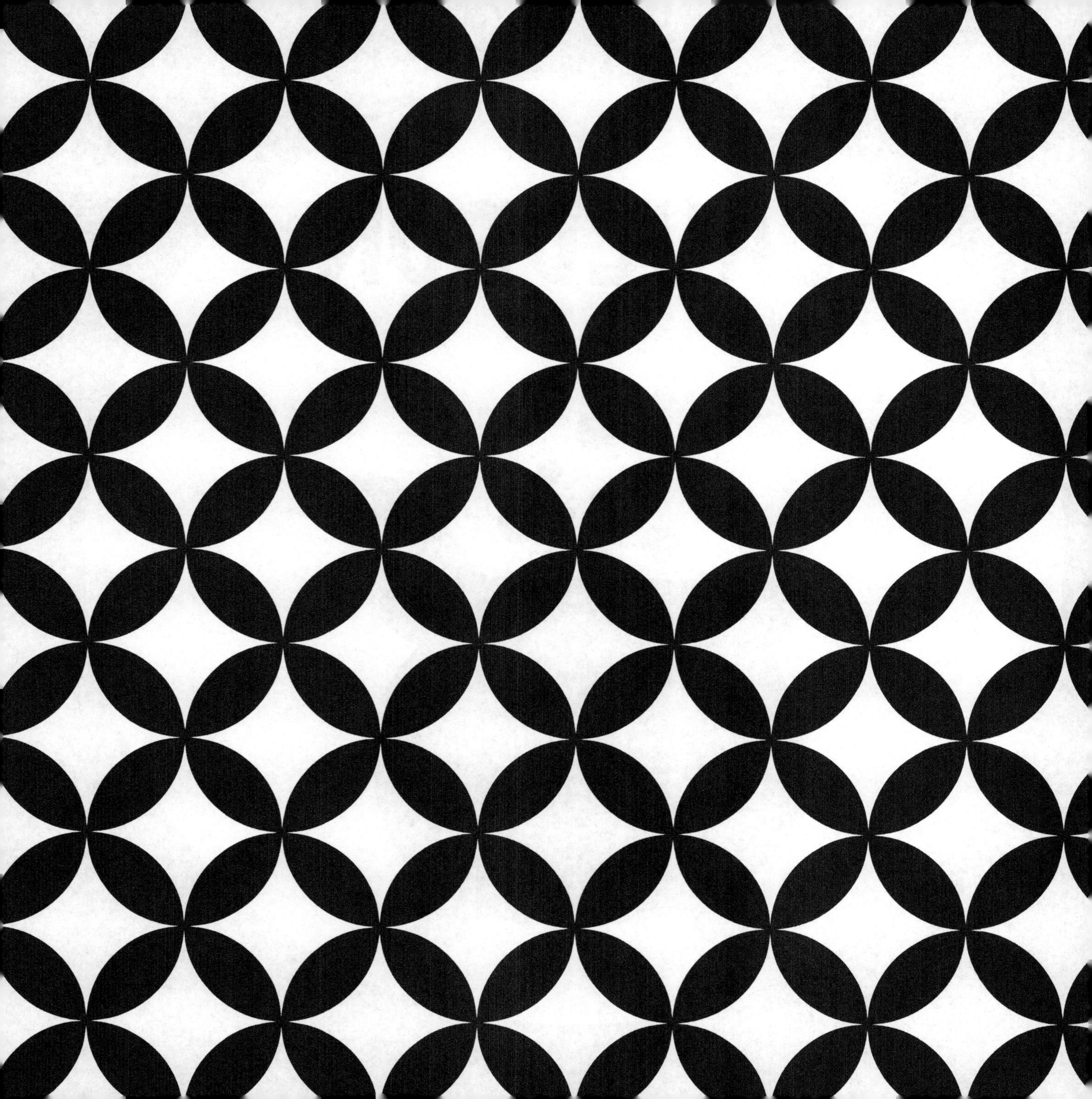

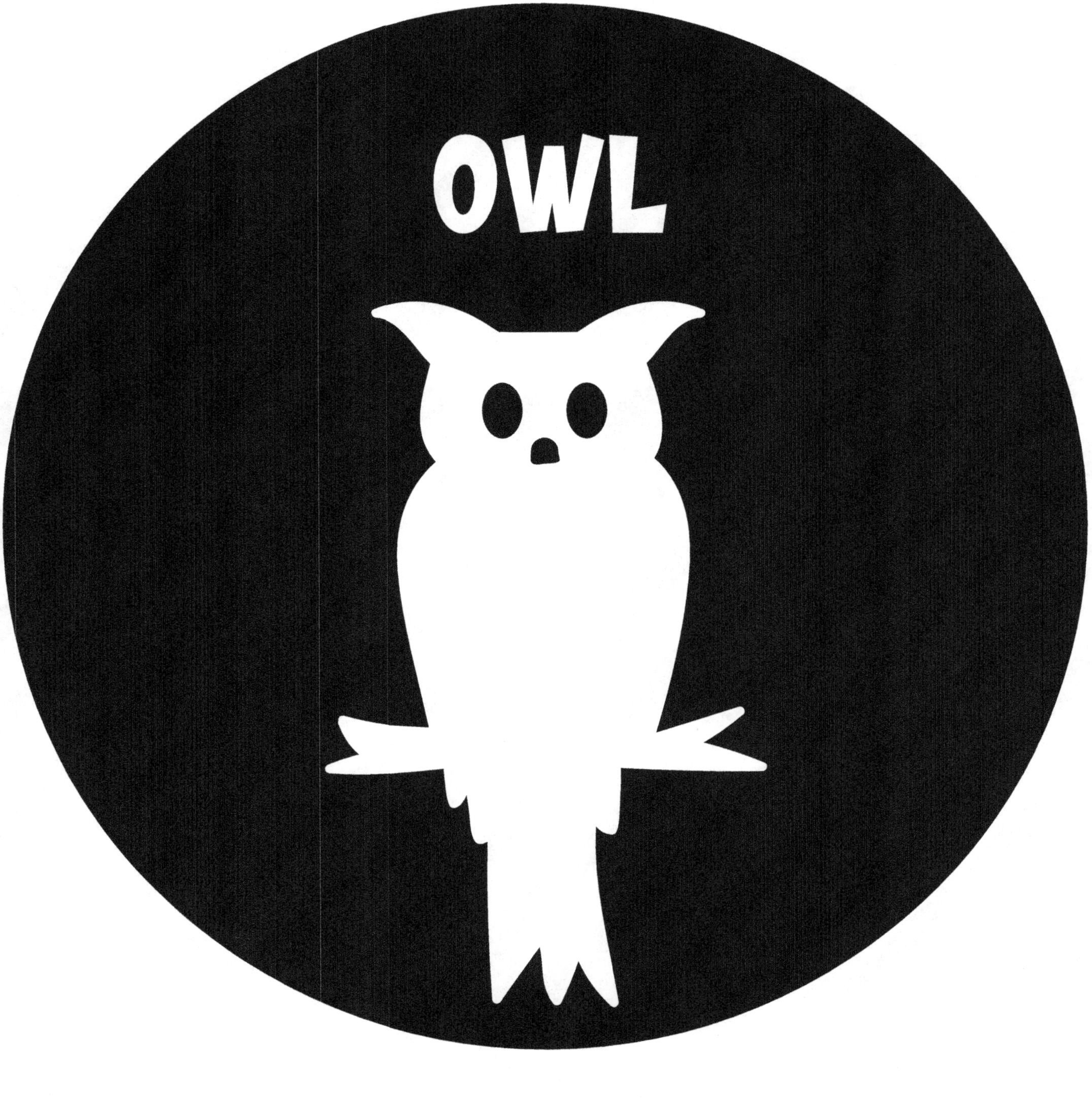
OWL

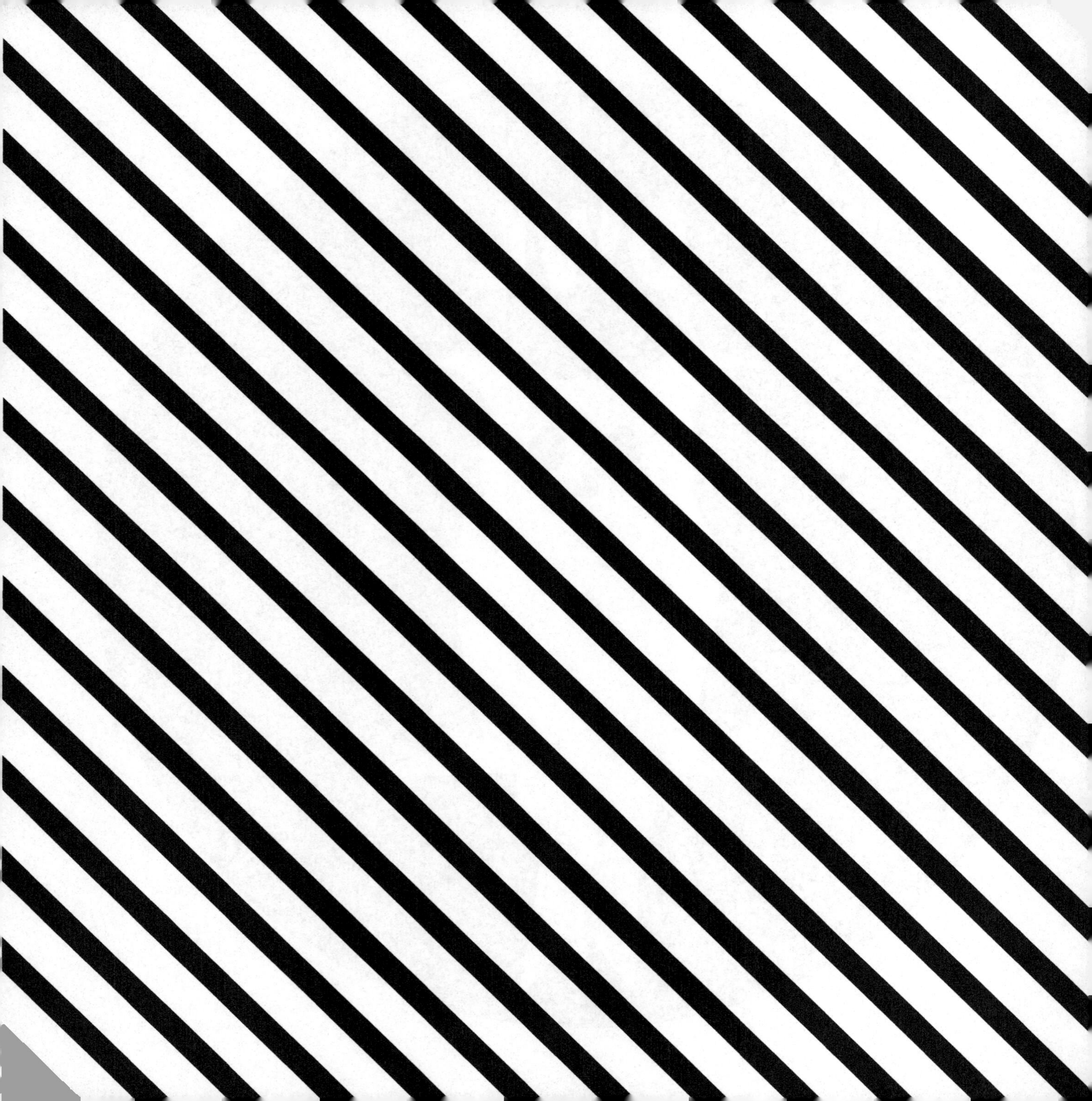

WITCH HAT

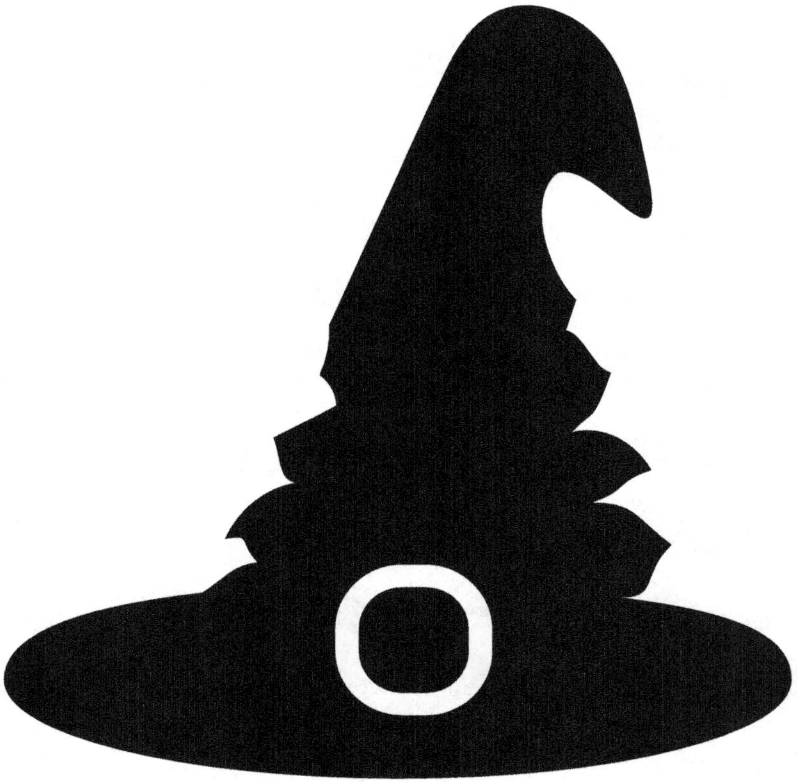

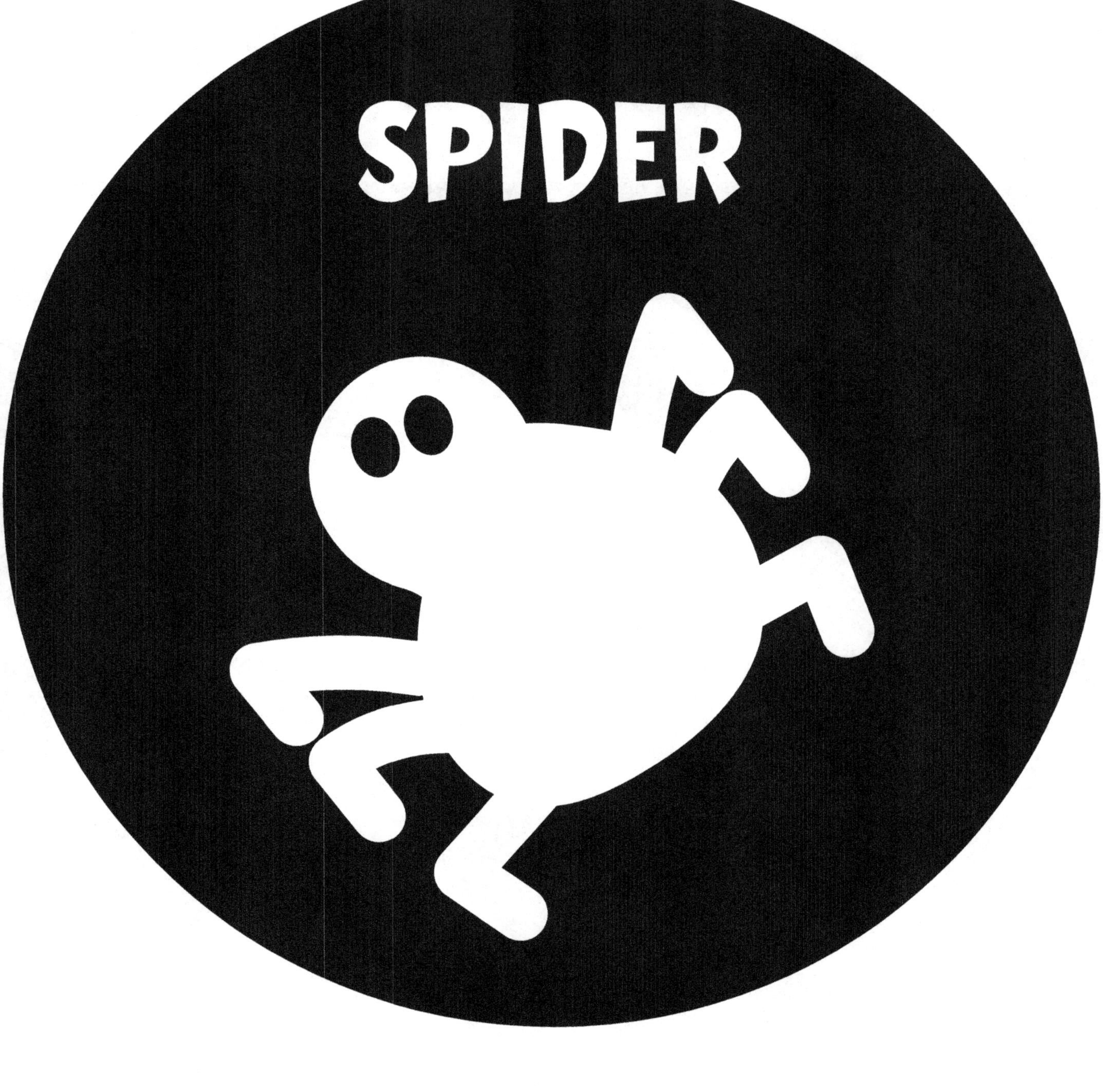
SPIDER

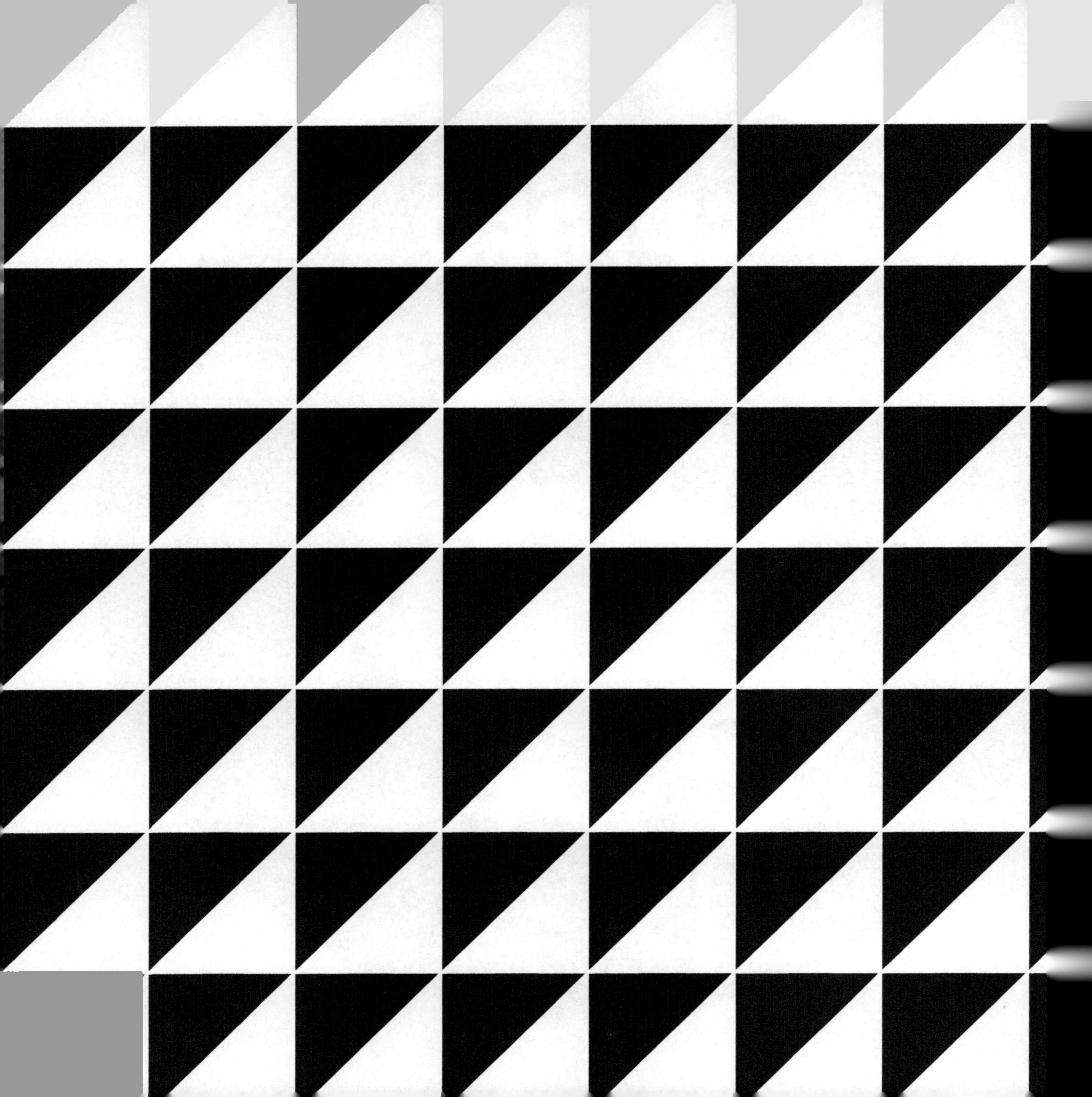

BAT

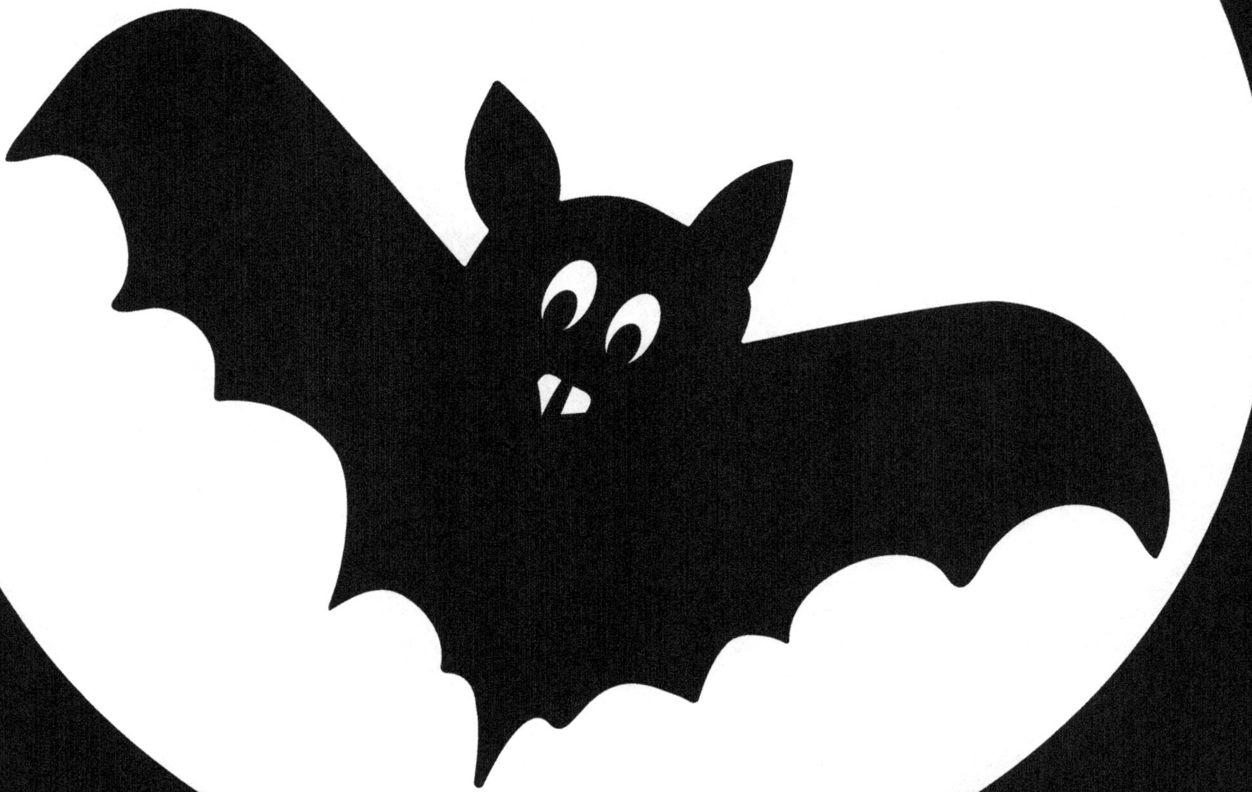

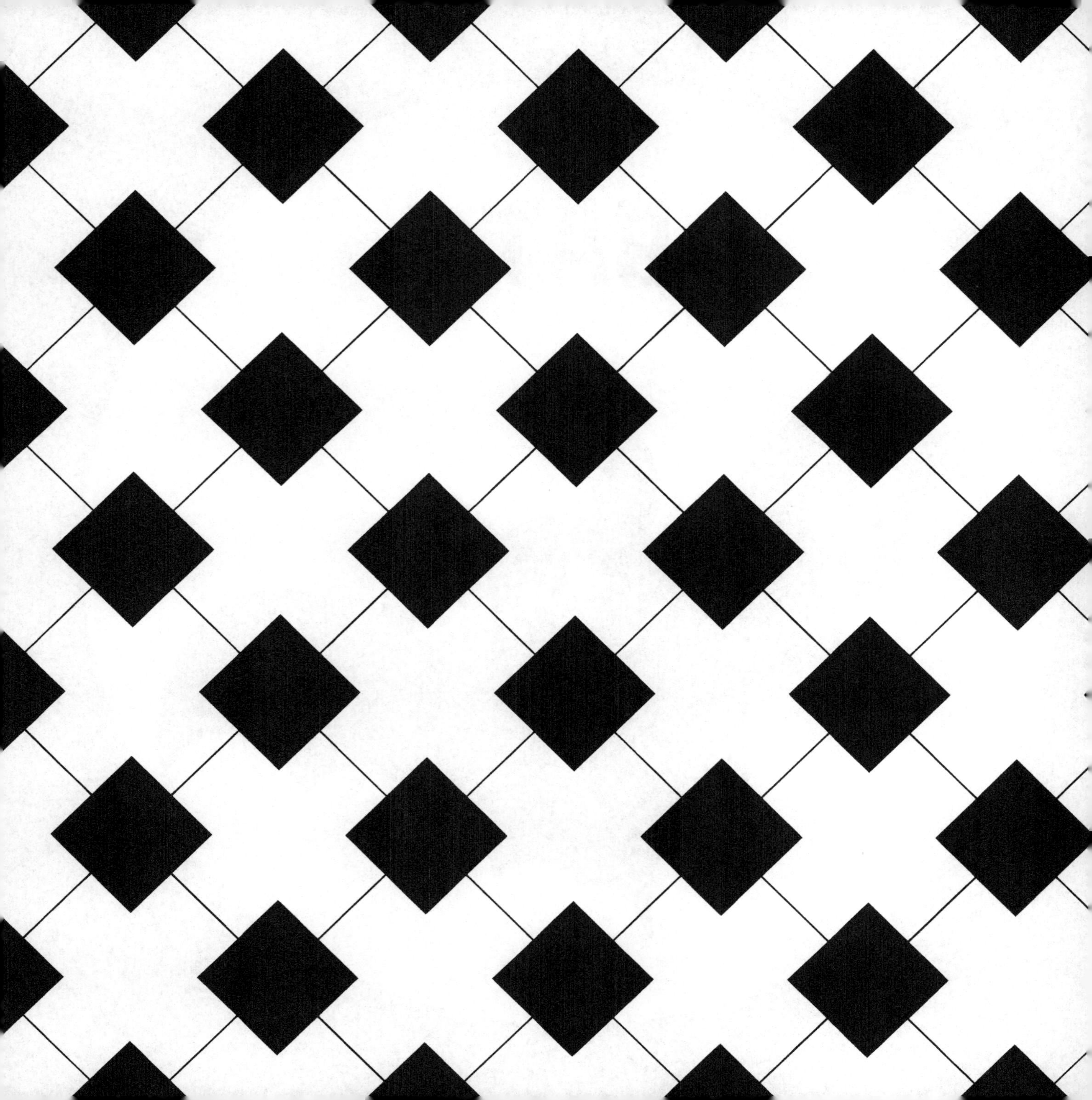

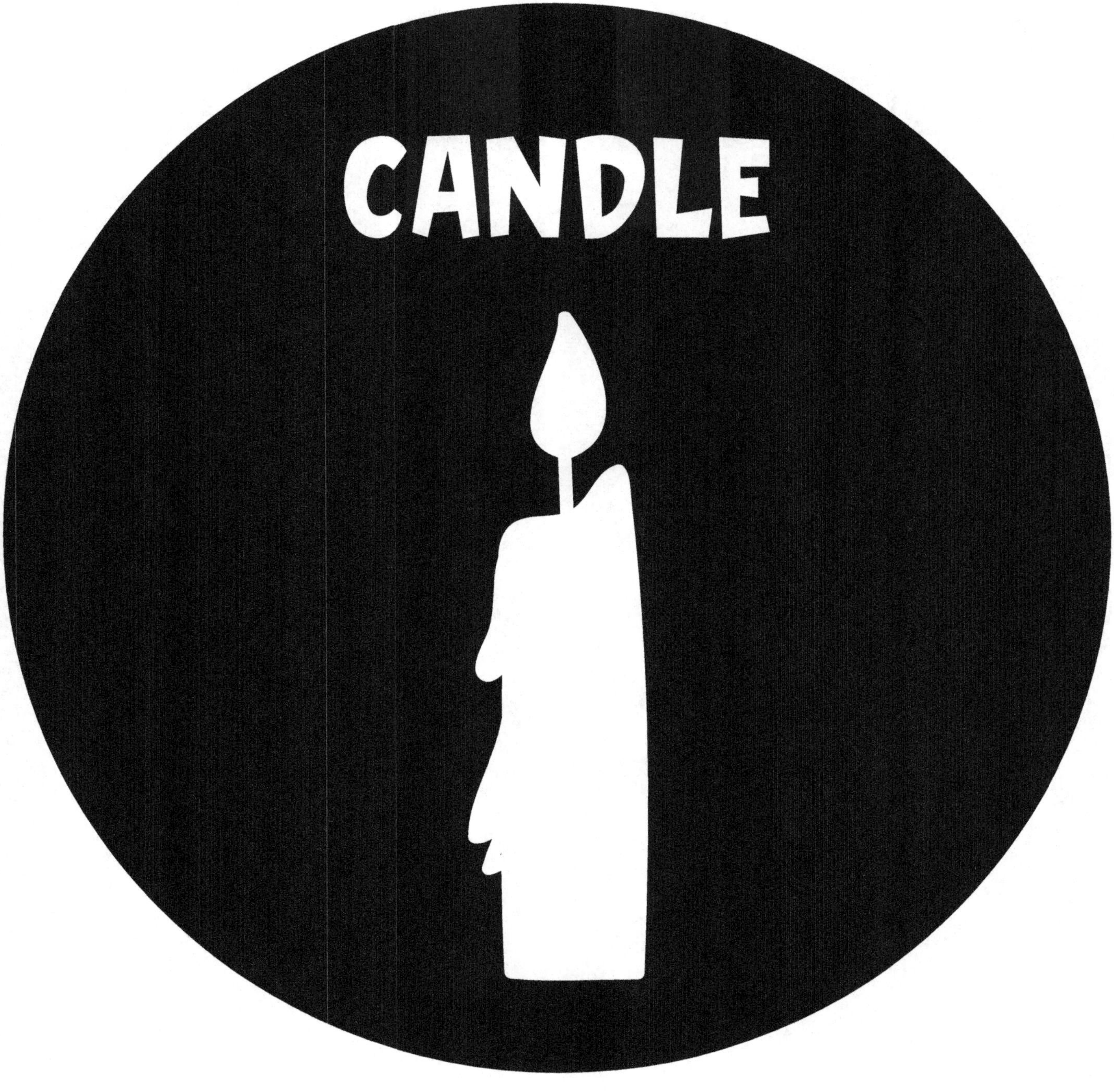
CANDLE

SKULL

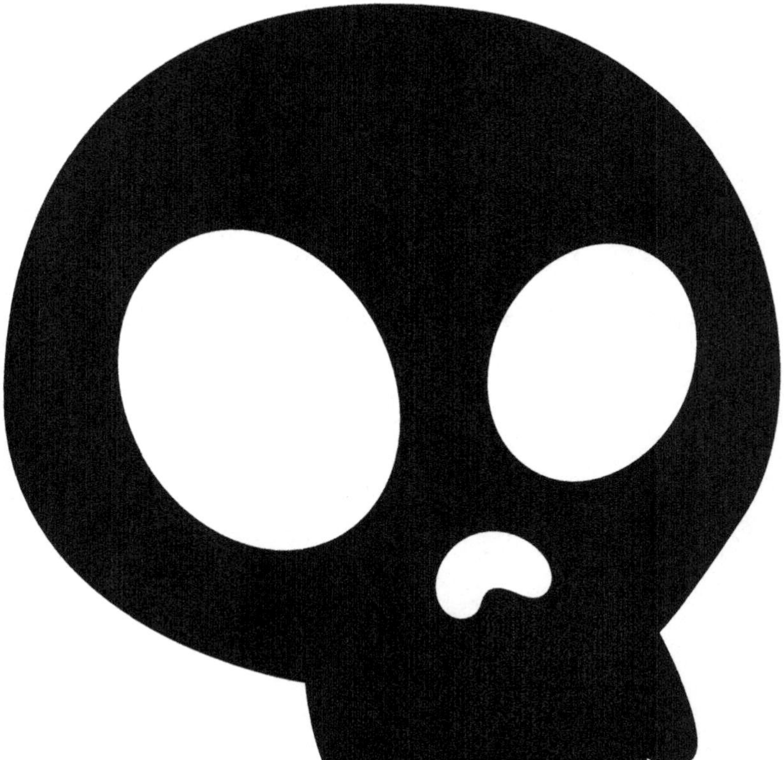

Your feedback is what keeps us going.

Please feel free to leave

an honest review on our Amazon page.